Books in the Linkers series

Homes discovered through Art & Technology
Homes discovered through Geography
Homes discovered through History
Homes discovered through Science

Myself discovered through Art & Technology
Myself discovered through Geography
Myself discovered through History
Myself discovered through Science

Toys discovered through Art & Technology
Toys discovered through Geography
Toys discovered through History
Toys discovered through Science

Water discovered through Art & Technology
Water discovered through Geography
Water discovered through History
Water discovered through Science

Food discovered through Art & Technology
Food discovered through Geography
Food discovered through History
Food discovered through Science

Journeys discovered through Art & Technology
Journeys discovered through Geography
Journeys discovered through History
Journeys discovered through Science

First published 1997 A&C Black (Publishers) Limited
35 Bedford Row, London WC1R 4JH

ISBN 0-7136-4760-4
A CIP catalogue record for this book is available from the British Library.

Copyright © 1997 BryantMole Books

Commissioned photographs by Zul Mukhida
Design by Jean Wheeler   Artwork by John Yates

Consultant: Hazel Grice

Acknowledgements

Cephas; Franck Auberson 4 (left), W. Geiersperger 5, Chapel Studios; Zul Mukhida 18 (both), 22/3, Bruce Coleman; Jane Burton 7 (left), Tony Stone Images; Renee Lynn 2, Lori Adamski Peek 14, James Wells 15 (right), Don Smetzer 16, Zefa; 3 (right), 6, 7 (right), 15 (left), 20.

Printed and bound in Italy by L.E.G.O.

Food

discovered through
Science

Karen Bryant-Mole

Contents

Why do we need
  food? 2
Plants 4
Animals 6
People 8
Types of food 10
Using food 12

Diet 14
Eating 16
Senses 18
Cooking 20
Safe food 22
Glossary 24
Index 24

A & C Black • London

Why do we need food?

Every living thing needs food.

Living things

There are two main groups of living things; animals and plants. Plants include things like trees, grasses and vegetables as well as wild flowers and garden plants.

In science, the word 'animal' does not just mean creatures such as lions or rabbits, it also includes human beings, fish and birds.

Growing

Food helps living things to grow and stay healthy. These puppies will need a lot of food because they have a lot of growing to do.
Puppies are very lively. Food gives them energy.

Dying

Without food and water, living things die.
This plant is dying because it does not have enough food.
Animals, including people, would also die without food.

3

Plants

Plants are special living things because almost all of them can make their own food.

Roots
Most plants have roots.
The roots grow downwards and suck up water from the soil all around the plant.
The water travels up to the plant's leaves, through thin tubes inside the plant.

Leaves are very important to a plant because they are where the plant's food is made.
The plant's leaves make food using sunlight, air and water from the soil.

Large plants

Large plants, such as trees, need a lot of food.
They have many leaves, so they can get as much sunlight and air as possible.
Their roots spread out a long way, so they can find plenty of water.

Animals

Every animal has certain foods it prefers to eat.

Plants or meat?
Some animals only
eat plants.
Plants include roots and
fruit as well as leaves.
Rabbits, sheep, giraffes
and koala bears are all
plant-eating animals.

Some animals, such as
lions and dogs, mainly
eat meat.
Other animals, like this
brown bear, eat both
plants and meat.

Wild animals

Wild animals have to find or catch their own food.

Many meat-eating animals catch their food by chasing and killing other animals.

But some, like the spider in the picture below, catch their dinner in a trap!

Pets

Pets do not have to worry about finding their own food.

People buy food for them.

If you have a pet, it is important to remember to feed it every day.

People

People like to eat a variety of different foods.

Plants
Some of our food comes from plants.
We eat different parts of plants.
When we eat lettuce or cabbage,
we are eating the plant's leaves.
When we eat carrots, we are eating
the plant's roots.

Animals
Some of our food comes from animals.
Pork, for instance, comes from pigs.
We get milk from cows and eggs from hens.
Some people choose not to eat food that
comes from animals.

Water

As well
as needing
food, all
living things
need water.
We get most of
the water we need from
drinks but some of it comes from food.
Strawberries, cucumbers, oranges and
celery all contain a lot of water.

9

Types of food

Food can be sorted into one of several different groups.

Vegetables
Vegetables are plants that have a part which can be eaten. Potatoes, broccoli and carrots are all types of vegetable.

Fruits
In science, the fruit is the part of a plant where a seed or seeds grow.
We usually use the word 'fruit' to mean foods such as apples and bananas.
But foods like tomatoes are fruits too.

Cereals

Cereals are the seeds from special grasses, such as wheat, rice or maize. They are used to make foods like breakfast cereals and flour.

Dairy products

The phrase 'dairy products' means milk and foods that are made from milk, such as cheese.

Meat and fish

Meat and fish are foods that come from animals.

Using food

Food helps our bodies in different ways.

Growing
Some foods are important because they
help our bodies to grow.
These foods include meat, fish,
eggs, cereals, cheese, beans
and milk.

Energy

We need energy to keep our bodies active.

Almost all foods give our bodies some energy but certain foods are better than others.

Potatoes, nuts, rice, sugar, milk, cheese and bread all give us lots of energy.

Vitamins and minerals

There are special chemicals, called vitamins and minerals, in most foods.

They have many jobs, such as helping our blood and skin to stay healthy and helping to build strong bones.

The foods in the picture on the left are good sources of different vitamins and minerals.

Diet

The sort of food we eat is called our diet.

Staying healthy
We need to eat the correct amount of the right types of food, so that we grow, have enough energy and stay healthy.
This is known as having a balanced diet.

Unhealthy diet

Some people eat too much of the wrong types of foods.

If people eat much more than their body needs, their body stores it as fat. Too much fat is unhealthy.

Needs

Different people need different amounts of food.

A growing teenager needs more food than an elderly person.

People who use a lot of energy in their work need more food than people who sit at a desk all day.

Eating

Our bodies have special parts that help us to eat and use food.

Chewing

You use your teeth to bite off pieces of food. You chew the food by grinding it between your back teeth.
As the food is chewed, it becomes mixed with saliva, or spit.
When the food has been chewed, your tongue pushes it towards your throat.

Inside your body

You swallow the food down a pipe in your throat, known as your gullet.

The food then travels through your body.

It passes through your stomach and then through the small intestine and the large intestine.

Your body takes out what it needs.

What it doesn't need, or has used, comes out when you go to the loo.

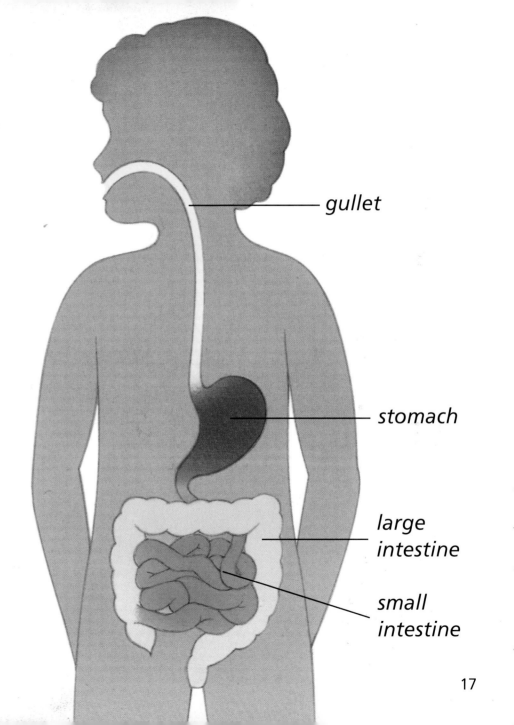

gullet

stomach

large intestine

small intestine

Senses

We have five senses, many of which we use when we eat food.

Taste
You use your tongue to taste your food. Your tongue is covered with taste-buds.

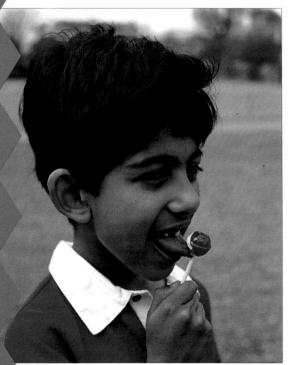

There are four groups of taste-buds. Each group recognises a different taste; sweet, sour, salty or bitter. The taste-buds on the tip of your tongue recognise a sweet taste.

Smell
You use your nose to smell your food. You can smell food while it is being prepared and when it is on the plate in front of you.
You also smell your food while you are eating it.

18

Sight, touch and hearing
You use your eyes to see and choose food.
You use your hands to touch and pick up food.
You can even hear some food, like this bowl of cereal!

Cooking

Many of the foods we eat are cooked before they are eaten.

Heating

We cook food by heating it.

Food can be heated using a variety of machines, including microwave ovens, gas cookers or electric cookers.

It can also be heated on a barbecue.

Food can be cooked in different ways, such as boiling, roasting, grilling or frying.

Changes

Cooking makes changes happen to food.

It can make hard foods, such as potatoes, softer.

It can turn soft bread into crisp toast.

It can change a runny mixture into a solid cake.

Cooked food

Once food has been cooked, it stays cooked.

This cake will cool down but it cannot become uncooked.

Safe food

The food we eat must be fresh.

Fresh food
These fresh tomatoes have shiny, tight skins.
Packaged food often has a 'Use by' date on it.
This date tells us when the food should be used by.

Bad food
Most foods, if left, will eventually go bad, or 'off'.
Sometimes we can see that food has gone off.
Sometimes we can smell that it is bad.
Eating food that has gone off is not good for our bodies.

Keeping food

Food that is kept cold in the fridge or frozen in the freezer will stay fresh for longer.

Food in tins has been treated in a special way. It stays good to eat for months or even years.

Why not look in your food cupboards at home and try to find the 'Use by' dates on tins, boxes and bottles?

Glossary

diet the food you usually eat
energy what makes things go or work
grinding rubbing together
healthy when your body is fit and well
intestine tube-like parts of your body
where changes are made to the food
you eat, so that your body can use it

minerals and **vitamins** important parts
of your food that your body has to
have to stay well
packaged put into packets, bags,
boxes, bottles or tins
roasting baking in an oven
taste-buds tiny bumps on your tongue
that help you to taste food

Index

animals 2, 3, 6–7, 8

cereals 11, 12
chewing 16
cooking 20–21

dairy products 11
diet 14–15
dying 3

eating 16–17
energy 3, 13, 15

fat 15
fish 11, 12

fresh food 22–23
fruits 6, 9, 10

growing 3, 12

health 13, 14, 15
heating 20

leaves 4, 5, 8

meat 6, 8, 11, 12
milk 11, 12, 13
minerals 13

people 7, 8–9
pets 7

plants 2, 3, 4–5, 6, 8

roots 4, 5, 6, 8

senses 18–19
smell 18
stomach 17

taste 18
teeth 16
trees 2, 5

vegetables 2, 8, 10
vitamins 13

water 3, 4, 5, 9

How to use this book

Each book in this series takes a familiar topic or theme and focuses on one area of the curriculum: science, art and technology, geography or history. The books are intended as starting points, illustrating some of the many different angles from which a topic can be studied. They should act as springboards for further investigation, activity or information seeking.

History
changes have taken place during the past one hundred years, relating to:
- the way food is produced
- how food is transported
- where and how food is bought
- the variety of food available
- the utensils used to prepare food
- how food is cooked
- where food is stored
- how food is preserved
- eating meals

Art and Technology
- food is prepared to make it taste good and look attractive
- chefs are creative with food
- some tools are especially designed for food
- food features in 'still life' works of art
- make a pizza
- design a menu
- print with food
- model a meal
- create a summer drink
- make a still life picture

FOOD
key concepts and activities explored within each book

Science
- all living things need food
- plants make their own food
- foods can be classified into different groups
- we need to eat a variety of foods
- our bodies use different types of food in different ways
- a healthy diet is important
- food travels through our digestive system
- smelling and tasting food involves our senses
- food changes when it is cooked or heated

Geography
- food is usually produced on farms
- there are different types of farm, where different types of food are produced
- climate and land-type determine the food produced
- food can be found in salt water and fresh water
- many foods are processed and packaged in factories
- food is sold in markets, supermarkets and shops
- food can be imported and exported